BACK THE F*CK UP!

DANNY VITTORE

Published by

Krause Publications, a division of F+W Media, Inc.
700 East State Street • Iola, WI 54990-0001
715-445-2214 • 888-457-2873
www.krausebooks.com

To order books or other products call toll-free 1-800-258-0929
or visit us online at *www.krausebooks.com*

Front cover photo copyright: Sergey Timofeev/Shutterstock. Back cover photo copyrights: cane toad, Dirk Ercken/Shutterstock; squirrel, Patrick Power/Shutterstock.

ISBN-13: 978-1-4402-2925-1
ISBN-10: 1-4402-2925-2

Cover design by Sharon Bartsch
Designed by Shawn Williams
Edited by Kristine Manty

Printed in China

ACKNOWLEDGMENTS

So many people to thank! As always, I would like to thank my parents for whom without, I wouldn't be here to write this book. Also, so many thanks to my editor, Kris Manty, for coming up with the idea and seeing it through the whole way even though I have been extremely tardy in my submissions (including this one!). Also, many thanks to friends for being around and supportive. Thanks to 1407, although you guys are probably a bit TOO enthusiastic. Thanks to the Workshop, Jack, DOB, Wong, Brockway, and all the others who helped me get a head start to be published and get known in the first place.

Thanks National Geographic, Discovery Channel, and Animal Planet for being informative, kind of, but seriously, I don't care what the statistics say, crabbing is not fun to watch. Thanks to Jimmy Kimmel for being afraid of animals (fake or real, doesn't matter, it's hilarious).

Lastly, of course, it would be silly of me to not thank all the crazy-ass animals that fill this book, for without them, this would be a much more boring world. Safer, but boring.

ABOUT THE AUTHOR

Humorist Danny Vittore has led a generally uneventful life. This is because, before July of 2010, Danny Vittore did not exist. However, his creator, David Dong, has been around since February 25, 1993. With such an unfortunate name, David has been the target of many dick jokes—therefore, he found it quite ironic when he, himself, became a purveyor of dick jokes on CRACKED.com in the summer of 2010. As an amateur writer, yet "master of sarcasm," David created Danny, who used his experiences of being the butt of dick jokes to write articles, including the Internet sensation this book is based on: "6 Animals That Just Don't Give a Fuck." Referred to as the Justin Bieber of blogging by forbes.com, Danny also writes for gamebreakers.co and is finishing his freshman year at New York University.

CONTENTS

WELL,
AFTER WE
ATE EVERY
LAST ANIMAL
ON THIS
PLANET,
WOOD IS
REALLY ALL
WE GOT...

INTRODUCTION

"HOLY FUCKING SHIT!!! RUN FOR YOUR LIVES!!!"

The above reaction just happens to not be the response that people give nowadays when they come across an animal, wild or otherwise. Instead, the most common response nowadays is utter and complete infatuation if the animal is at all fat and cute like a panda, or a bizarre fascination if it's something a tad more dangerous like a tiger or a hippo. Yes, hippopotamuses. *They are dangerous.* Right now, you are probably thinking to yourself, "Ha-ha! That's hilarious. They couldn't possibly hurt us! They are so awfully FAT. And CUTE!" As you will soon find out, fatness and cuteness mean jack shit to how dangerous an animal can be.

But before we delve into individual animals, it's probably worth figuring out why we, as human beings, no longer share the same fear of most animals that our cave-dwelling ancestors possessed. There are many extremely plausible answers, but the one that I believe is the real culprit starts with *video games*. In 2006, a study by Iowa State University concluded that seeing and performing violent acts in video games could make subjects desensitized to real-life violence.

> **Fatness and cuteness mean jack shit to how dangerous an animal can be.**

Surely this idea of desensitization can permeate through to the perception of animals, especially since the magical box known as the television is completely inundated with all things bestial. Kids nowadays grow up with movies like *Finding Nemo*, where there are a bunch of sharks who are "vegetarian" and against violence, as well as the *Madagascar* series, where there are friendly talking lions, zebras, giraffes, and hippos all living together in perfect harmony. Then there are things like the *Chronicles of Narnia*, where one of the main heroes is a huge talking lion that seems to give free hugs to children without finding the need to bite their

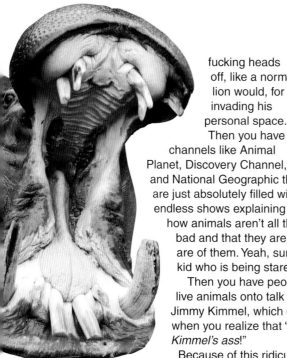

fucking heads off, like a normal lion would, for invading his personal space.

Then you have channels like Animal Planet, Discovery Channel, and National Geographic that are just absolutely filled with endless shows explaining how animals aren't all that bad and that they are really more scared of you than you are of them. Yeah, sure. Try telling that to an 8-year-old kid who is being stared down upon by a grizzly bear.

Then you have people like Dave Salmoni, who bring live animals onto talk shows to scare the living shit out of Jimmy Kimmel, which only makes it all the more hilarious when you realize that "that hornbill could totally *kick Kimmel's ass*!"

Because of this ridiculous saturation of animal love (probably caused by Greenpeace or PETA or something) even quintessentially scary animal movies, like *Jaws*, are becoming more hilarious than frightful.

This is, of course, the opposite of what should happen. People shouldn't see a squirrel and think, "Awwwh! It's so cute! Let's give it a peanut!" They should really be thinking, "I need to keep my distance!" These are wild, *unpredictable* animals we are talking about. *Not petting zoo exhibits*!

> **People shouldn't see a squirrel and think, 'Awwwh! It's so cute! Let's give it a peanut!' They should really be thinking, 'I need to keep my distance!'**

Damn you Dave Salmoni, Discovery Channel, *Narnia*, and National Geographic for warping our minds!

So in summary, damn you Dave Salmoni, Discovery Channel, *Narnia*, and National Geographic for warping our minds!!! We have become too used to sitting in the comfort of our home cinemas, living rooms or whatnot, watching animals do whatever the fuck animals like to do without realizing that we are giving ourselves a false sense of security so that the next time we see a raccoon we wouldn't think twice about any possible danger—that is until it walks over to you and *gives you rabies*. Safari guides don't carry a big-ass gun around with them just because they like the workout.

And without further ado, I believe it would be pertinent to go into depth what brought upon this explosion of mildly angry words on a page. Namely, if you have somehow not read the title of this book, well ...

ANIMALS DON'T GIVE A SHIT!

There are so many shits they couldn't give, it's ridiculous. Seriously.

Chimps are not the friendly creatures Jane Goodall would want us to believe. They eat BABIES.

ANTS

Ants are the first animal you will read about in this book. Don't think this makes them less give-a-shittable because most lists go from least crazy to craziest. No, this book is alphabetical; ants could be number one, or plain chump change. Depends on your perspective I suppose. Although I have to say, if you think ants are chump change, you must be one *crazy* mother. Why you may ask? You kill ants all the time, right? With magnifying glasses and the soles of your boots, right? Sometimes you

This ant has got to be some crazy shit for scientists to just give up and call it 'crazy.'

gas your whole house to get them out and hire professional killers to get at them. If the need to perform holocaustic genocide with assassins just to keep their numbers in check isn't enough to prove to you how crazy ants are, then the fact that they keep coming back for more has got to. No? Well, what about the *crazy ant*?

That's right, there is an ant called the crazy ant. This ant has got to be some crazy shit for scientists to just give up and call it "crazy." As a point of reference, there is a species known as bullet ants, who shriek like banshees and jump off tree branches onto you to sting you with the most painful sting you will encounter in the insect kingdom. All of this because you might be a little too close to their obscured-by-leaves-and-high-up-in-a-tree-and-you-had-no-idea-it-was-there ant hive. The crazy ant has got to be able to top that kind of crazy somehow. And it does so by twitching and moving erratically when disturbed. Also by taking over landmasses—like *supervillains*.

The crazy ants are invading just about everywhere, but the place they are having the most impact upon is Christmas Island. Although severely lacking in Santa Claus and other things in the Christmas department, what the island does have are millions upon millions of crabs. The ants (brought upon the island by sheer human mistake) took it upon themselves to rid the world of crabs. They did so by creating

ONE CRAB DOWN, A FEW MILLION TO GO!

multiple super-colonies, which can be miles across from which they fan out and eat whatever crabs (or thing) they can find. And for some near inexplicable reason, crabs seem to be steroids to the ants, making them bigger and stronger than they used to be, and they just don't stop conquering more land.

Every piece of land that becomes part of the crazy ant empire never leaves their hand-feet-antennae things and becomes completely desolate wastelands devoid of all life except bacteria. This probably shows an extreme level of misjudgment among these super-ants because what will they eat once they've eaten everything? Themselves? Probably, but I think they know that when they run out of crabs to eat, they can just form those massive inter-ant-body floats that ants have been known to make, and sail across the vast oceans to invade more plentiful lands, like California, until they have WORLD DOMINATION. I think it would be wise to stock up on flamethrowers and napalm right about now.

> **It would be wise to stock up on flamethrowers and napalm right about now.**

STEVENS! HOLD UP THE SCREW PROPERLY!

A HORROR HORDE OF CRAWL-AND-CRUSH GIANTS CLAWING OUT OF THE EARTH'S STEAMING DEPTHS!

NO MENACE LIKE IT KNOWN TO MAN OR BEAST BEFORE!

This city is under martial law until we annihilate THEM!

THE M

"THEM!" JAMES WHITMORE · EDMUND GWENN · JOAN WELDON · JAMES ARNESS

WARNER BROS.

©2004 HeritageGalleries.com

WE WELCOME OUR NEW INSECT OVERLORDS.

There are so many different kinds of ants and the crazy shit they do could fill up its own book, but a quick rundown will let you know that there is a kind of ant that literally explodes itself on any plausible threat to protect the colony, whilst there is another species that knows how to fucking farm. Fucking farming, that's a people thing! Also there is another species that invades the colony of an entirely different species of ants, massacres them, steals their young, and enslaves them to do their bidding. If ants have so little respect for similar beings, I don't like to think what they would do to beings that have stepped on them, burned them, and gassed them for years. Shit.

ARCHER FISH

The archer fish isn't an archer in the sense that it has hands and arms with which it can grasp a bow and arrow and hit a bull's-eye from 50 yards. That would be stupid. Preposterous even. No, it just shoots water at you at an extremely high velocity—very accurately.

This method is in fact how the archer fish gains its sustenance. For you see, the archer fish eats insects. Not content with mere water boatman and other marine-dwelling insects, the archer fish has decided to evolve a special jaw that allows them to shoot jets of water, quite accurately, *up to 15 feet*. It's important

> **The fish just literally spit on physics like it ain't no thing.**

The archer fish has decided to evolve a special jaw that allows them to shoot jets of water, quite accurately, up to 15 feet.

to note that these little fishies are mostly around 3 inches long, which makes 15 feet quite a significantly large distance.

Of course, like most things, practice makes perfect and they start learning to shoot when they are only about an inch long. They practice until they are adults, when they are then able to hit spiders, grasshoppers, and butterflies accurately on the *first try*. Of course, mostly it's about hitting the bug so that it loses its perch on an overhanging branch over a body of water and thus falling into the water to be eaten. However, the jets of water are so powerful, they have been known to kill the bugs immediately.

You are now probably thinking, "Pshht! So a fish can shoot things outside of water. What's the big deal?" Clearly, the fact that these archer fish have been able to circumvent the protection that we land creatures like to call "air" with projectiles has just gone over your head. But what about the fact that they can calculate mathematics and the laws of physics near instantaneously? Archer fish are able to find the exact angle they need to hit targets outside the water, keeping in account the *laws of refraction*. That's right, these fish can calculate refraction and it's not even like they are in perfectly clear water. It's murky river water. But the fish just literally spit on physics like it ain't no thing and calculate the trajectory extremely quickly and get their lunch regardless. No word yet on their progress with Superstring Theory, though.

The shit's about to go down, quite literally.

BARNACLE GEESE

What would you take for granted? Gravity? Unconditional love from your parents? If not unconditional love from your parents, at least the feeling that your parents are looking out for your security and do their utmost so that you won't jump out of upper-floor windows or anything? That shit don't fly if you happen to be a barnacle goose gosling.

MMMMMMM. GRASS.

Barnacle geese only take the parenting thing halfway.

You see, barnacle geese are pretty ordinary geese, except for the fact that they nest on high, sheer cliffs. There's a good reason for this, though. The cliffs help to protect the goslings from dangerous predators such as the Arctic fox and the polar bear. So okay, so far they seem to give a lot of shits. However, as you may have deduced from the mention of gravity, upper-floor windows, and high sheer cliffs, the shit's about to go down, quite literally.

You see, barnacle geese only take the parenting thing halfway. Sure, they keep

> **They have most likely only been hatched for no more than a week and are forced to jump onto rocks—where Arctic foxes have been known to wait for this literal rain of food.**

them safe, but the other thing is that they just outright *refuse to feed their young*, which can sort of be seen as shooting yourself in the foot, since you've kept your babies alive long enough to just starve to death. Not to worry, though, for the barnacle geese have come up with a cunning plan to make their goslings get sustenance: *Force them to jump out of the nests and fall multiple stories and hope they don't get crushed by the rocks at the bottom.* Obviously.

Sure, lots of bird species force their young to jump out of nests, but most of these nests are really low and close to the ground. If they aren't, then the parents make sure that the places where their chicks will land are soft with leaves or feathers or something. Usually, such actions are done to convince the chicks to learn to fly through crisis. These chicks are obviously relatively mature and well fed up until that point. Not the goslings of the barnacle geese. They have most likely only been hatched for no more than a week and are forced to jump onto rocks—where Arctic foxes have been known to wait for this literal rain of food—with only their smallness and puffiness keeping them safe; aka, not really.

If the baby geese can get through this hellish baptism, which includes psyching oneself for suicide, crippling injuries, and foxes, only then will the goslings be able to eat the main staple of the barnacle geese: delicious, delicious *grass*.

BOLAS SPIDERS

In general, when animals start using tools, humans become fascinated and note that it shows certain animals are much more intelligent then they seem. Look! A chimpanzee is using a stick to poke at an anthill! It's practically human! And over there! A monkey is using a large rock to crack open nuts! Humanity's grasp as the only advanced and intelligent species on the planet is dooooooooooomed! Well, naysayers, we up the pot with a tint of badassery: The bolas spider, the Indiana Jones of the animal kingdom.

The bolas spider is what you would get if you mated Indiana Jones with a ninja.

By the "Indiana Jones" of the animal kingdom, I don't mean they raid tombs or constantly say things should belong in museums, and neither do they have a tendency to be chased by bizarrely large and round rocks. They also don't wear hats. But they do the one thing that everybody loves Indy for: whipping. And we don't mean weird kinky stuff in bed, although that would explain why Indy is with a different woman in every movie, but for more useful tasks, like *catching flies out of the air*.

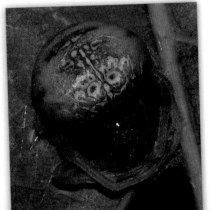

One day, the bolas spider decided to be hygienic (or probably lazy) and not spread its sticky-ass threads (spider web threads) all over the place. However, like most living organisms, it needed to eat, so it must have thought to itself, "Well, I guess I can just make a length of thread and use it as a whip to catch flying insects straight out of the air." It promptly did it. For anyone who's ever tried killing flies with rolled-up newspapers, you know it's difficult to do so and you probably need to be nearly a ninja to catch them. Now imagine your newspaper was so thin you can barely see it. You probably can't even imagine the difficulty. *You'd probably need to be two and a half ninjas*!

Okay, so I made a mistake. The bolas spider is what you would get if you mated Indiana Jones with a ninja, and when the offspring turned out to be a spider, you forced the spider only to use its spider webs as whips and gave it no purpose in life other than to **eat**.

BOMBARDIER BEETLES

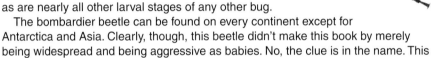

The bombardier beetle has a badass name and rightly so—it is a pretty badass animal, even if it is a bug and you can kill it with a boot. Carnivorous to the exoskeleton, bombardier beetles hunt other insects for sustenance, and they start doing so from the *larval stage*. These guys are born vicious. In comparison, ants are pathetic, near helpless, blobs as larva, as are nearly all other larval stages of any other bug.

The bombardier beetle can be found on every continent except for Antarctica and Asia. Clearly, though, this beetle didn't make this book by merely being widespread and being aggressive as babies. No, the clue is in the name. This beetle's ass is a cannon. *Literally*.

The ass cannon located on the abdomen of the bombardier beetle is truly a marvel of the animal kingdom. Not only does it spew an extremely potent mixture of chemicals at 212 degrees Fahrenheit (which can kill insects on touch and severely injure larger creatures like us), it shoots it in 70 extremely fast and successive shots like a mini-gun, *but faster*. It doesn't take much provocation to make these guys shoot at you. Look at it funny and your eyes are liquid.

The chemical and physical processes that occur within the beetle to heat up the liquid and then quickly spew it out is unmatched by any modern technology. In fact, scientists and engineers are desperately trying to emulate this in machines. But quite frankly, we don't got shit on these guys.

This beetle's ass is a cannon. *Literally*.

CANE TOADS

Australia is famous for having many weird and/or dangerous animals on different levels of not-give-a-shittery. Most of them just turned out that way, but what would you expect if you were native to the international land of scary shit?

Cane toads would probably rape your hand if you kept it too close to them for too long.

Interestingly enough, though, you can't actually blame Australia for cane toads, but you can totally blame *the Australians* for bringing them to Australia to eat bugs that were destroying their crops. The cane toads decided that was a stupid thing to do and promptly started to destroy Australian wildlife. Big wildlife fail there from the Australians.

As a result, cane toads have spread like wildfire throughout Australia. In fact, they are so widespread, they are considered pests and some people find it is their God-given duty to actually drive off the road in order to squash a toad or two. If they are on the road itself, well, easy pickings! These dead, run-over toads leave some toad pancakes on the road, which, as you can imagine, is not the prettiest sight in the world.

But being a reason for potential road accidents is not an extremely compelling reason to have cane toads in this book. Nope, the reason they are considered to not give a shit is because they perform a thing called Davian behavior, e.g. animal necrophilia. That's right: cane toads have been known to bump uglies with other dead cane toads ... and dead amphibians ... and just other dead things. In general, they are really horny bastards. They would probably rape your hand if you kept it too close to them for too long. Although it is quite disgusting, it would also be painful because of the fact that they secrete toxins.

The icing of the cake is the fact that one cane toad was caught in a documentary fucking the shit out of a dead cane toad. It just happened to be that a jeep flattened

BACK THE F*CK UP!

CLEARLY SOMETHING IS WRONG: THE TOAD BEING HUMPED IS STILL ALIVE.

this certain dead cane toad earlier, but clearly the cane toad didn't give a shit and continued the love ... *for 8 hours.*

CASSOWARIES

Speaking of Australia, what do you think is the most dangerous animal there? Some may say the infamous crocodile. Some may say the stingray, since one of them killed the freaking *Crocodile Hunter* for Christ's sake. I, however, think it's safe to say that the most dangerous animal in Australia is the cassowary.

The cassowary isn't just an Australian problem; it is in the *Guinness World Records* as the most dangerous bird on Earth. They have been known to outflank and attack human hunters, although hunters are unlikely to be hunting cassowary for food (or any other reason). The reason for this was elucidated when Australian administrative officers stationed in New Guinea were advised that cassowary "should be cooked with a stone in the pot: when the stone is ready to eat, so is the cassowary."

What makes cassowaries more frightening is the straight-up fact that they aren't afraid of humans, *especially* humans with guns. During World War II, American and Australian troops stationed in New Guinea were warned to stay away from *cassowaries*. Let's read that again: fully grown men, probably the most badass of the badass, with guns, fighting back waves and waves of terrifying Japanese banzai charges, were essentially told to run away like little girls when they see a cassowary.

Why all the fear? Because a kick from one of these guys can *disembowel a grown man or dog*. They also like eating snakes because *fuck snakes*. They have dagger-like claws on their feet, which aren't really the stabby-type, but for

> **Fully grown men, probably the most badass of the badass, with guns, fighting back waves and waves of terrifying Japanese banzai charges, were essentially told to run away like little girls when they see a cassowary.**

| BACK THE F*CK UP!

slashing—causing deep, quite fatal, wounds.

Zookeepers who take care of cassowaries have been interviewed doing their job. These are the men who take care of and feed the cassowaries, but at the mere sight of them, even near the entrance to their exhibit, the cassowaries (barely adults) started to attack the fencing with bloodlust to get at the zookeepers. Common equipment you will find on the cassowary zookeepers' arsenal includes riot shields and many, many rakes. One zookeeper even mentions how he would prefer to be in with the "5m long crocs than with the cassowary." Because, all of a sudden, crocodiles are pussies.

The zookeepers had many stories about cassowaries, but the following is my favorite one: "One of the most recent attacks was on a lady down at a small beach just south of here, picnicking with her family. Cassowaries went up, noticed that she had food, and got very aggressive. Now [the family] took the warning signs and hopped into a car. A cassowary actually jumped up and *sliced down her door*."

No more details were given after that. Not even fucking *metal* can put these guys off.

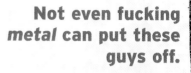

Not even fucking *metal* can put these guys off.

CATERPILLARS

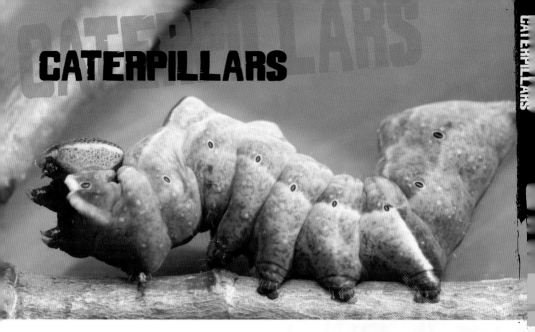

How do you view the caterpillar? A fat worm, sometimes fuzzy, sometimes not. Cute to some, gut-wrenchingly horrifying to others. All it does is eat leaves and fruit. Maybe you think all caterpillars are fat and speak in a German accent.

But the general consensus is that they are lazy, fat, useless organisms. Lazy and fat, maybe, but useless is not quite the word I would use to describe them. It turns out, caterpillars are masters at fraudulent behavior that can rival the movie, *Catch Me If You Can*, and Wall Street bankers.

On the scale of fraud, the following caterpillar is

> **Caterpillars are masters at fraudulent behavior that can rival Wall Street bankers.**

OUR DISGUISES
ARE SO AWESOME!
WHAT ARE WE
DRESSED UP AS?
UM...

actually quite honest and known as a myrmecophilous caterpillar. These caterpillars are usually herded and tended to by ants for the sweet secretions that these caterpillars give out when given a certain massage. The ants carry these "cows" out to graze and when they are done, they are brought back to safety in the colony. The symbiosis is so complete, that these two creatures are able to communicate quite well with mere vibrations. What the ants don't know is that the caterpillars are spiking the secretions with certain chemicals that keep the ants addicted to the secretions, thus cementing the ants' need to keep the caterpillars safe.

> **The caterpillar promptly starts eating its 'brothers and sisters' because fuck 'em, it was adopted anyway!**

But the ante can be upped with caterpillars. The specific species I'm interested in are myrmecophagous caterpillars, aka ant-eating caterpillars. Yes. Fucking. Carnivorous. *Caterpillars*. These caterpillars have evolved the ability to secrete certain pheromones to convince ants that

ALL HAIL THE HYPNO...PILLAR?

they are *ant larvae*. Ants, realizing they somehow misplaced a large larva outside of their colony for some silly reason, bring it back in together with the other ant larvae. The caterpillar promptly starts eating its "brothers and sisters" because fuck 'em, it was adopted anyway!

Another caterpillar takes it to an even *higher* level. It mimics the sounds and pheromones made by *queen ants* and are from then on treated like damned *royalty*. If the colony is attacked, the caterpillar "queen" is the first to be taken to safety over the *young*. And in times of famine, the worker ants have been known to feed larvae, *their babies*, to the "queen." The caterpillar doesn't give a shit; it's getting a free meal, again and again, and again. What makes it even more insane, is that in a controlled experiment, queen ants were put together with the faker and they saw through the facade and immediately attacked the caterpillar. The worker ants weren't having any of that shit, though, and *promptly started stinging and biting their actual queens.*

CHIMPANZEES

> **They share 95 percent of their genes with us and that's probably why they are fucked up.**

Chimpanzees? Not the CHIMPS, TOO! HOW CAN THEY BE ANYTHING SHORT OF ADORABLE?!?! Well, sorry to burst your collective bubbles, but chimpanzees are far from the friendly creatures Jane Goodall would want you to believe. Sure, they share 95 percent of their genes with us

Also, they eat _babies_. Yes, you read that right. They eat babies.

THEY HAVE GUNS NOW. WE'RE DOOMED!

(humans, just in case you are reading this from some future planet of the apes world and are also a gorilla), and that's probably why they are fucked up.

First of all, they _declare war_ on each other. War. No kidding. Male chimpanzees have been known to venture out of their territories in single file. And there isn't any normal ape fuckery going around, either. It is real stealthy Solid Snake stuff (without the cardboard box bullshit). Their objective? Expand the tribe's territory and fuck up any other chimpanzees that they encounter.

But like humanity, war isn't just about killing people who are different from you, there's killing your own as well! _Civil wars_

> **Holy shit. All of a sudden, *Rise of the Planet of the Apes* doesn't sound so stupid and far-fetched anymore.**

occur in chimpanzee societies as well. In a studied community of chimpanzees, a group of dissident chimps broke off from the original, and through time and repeated attacks, the rebel group eventually *annihilated* the original group!

That social thing was just the icing on the cake. Chimps are avid tool users. Right now you might be thinking, "Oh yeah! I know about that. Chimps use stones they find to bash open nuts or something and sticks to dig at termite mounds! It's interesting, but not terribly horrifying!" Well, what if I told you that they Bear Grylls it up a bit and manufacture spears, sharpened with their teeth, to spear bushbabies (a species of primates smaller than chimpanzees) to eat? Holy fuckeroons, they have **weapons**.

Also, they eat *babies.* Yes, you read that right. They eat babies. And we aren't just talking about chimp babies; they probably pull that shit all the time. There have been many reported instances when chimpanzees have taken *human babies* and then, well, people assume they **hate humans** and ate them, but I like to think they are just raising their own army of Tarzans that they will one day use to overthrow the oppressive humans because *fuck us.*

Did I mention that chimps are also extremely **intelligent**? Whilst most of the animal kingdom prides individuals who are large and strong, in chimp communities, the alpha male is the one who is the most *manipulative and politically intelligent.* Chimp males who have ambitions make allies who in the future will help them rise to dominance. Chimps are also able to learn sign language and symbols to communicate. **Holy shit**. All of a sudden, *Rise of the Planet of the Apes* doesn't sound so stupid and far-fetched anymore. Chimps can make weapons, are intelligent, and hate humans. This is a call to all crazy scientists out there: If you are making some sort of serum to boost intelligence, *stop giving it to chimpanzees!*

SURE, HUMANS AND CHIMPS ARE LIVING IN HARMONY NOW, BUT WE MAY ONE DAY SOON ALL BE LIKE CHARLTON HESTON AND SCREAMING, "IT'S A MADHOUSE ... A MADHOUSE!"

REAL
ROADRUNNERS
BEAR LITTLE
RESEMBLANCE
TO THE FAMOUS
ROAD RUNNER.

CUCKOOS

What do YOU know about the cuckoo bird? Don't worry, I'm going to be here forever (or at least until the pages rot away) and have all the time in the world. Dig into the deepest recesses of your mind. Go deeper. DEEPER! I bet (unless you're an ornithologist) that you know nada, nothing, diddly squat, about the cuckoo bird other than the fact that some wooden versions live in clocks and come out every hour to go "cuckoo."

The roadrunner will grab its prey and slam it on the ground until compliance is met.

The term "cuckoo" is actually a family of birds that includes such illustrious creatures like koels, couas, anis, and other seemingly random amalgamations of vowels and consonants. But a properly famous one is the Road Runner. Yup, old Mr. "meep meep" himself. Roadrunners are, unsurprisingly, not Woody Woodpecker-colored, aka blue. They are more boring and brown. But don't let this fashion incompetence fool you; roadrunners are ballsy.

They are able to fly, but almost always choose *not to*, because they can. Being able to run up to 20 miles per hour certainly does help. It also helps that they can eat anything from mice, insects, centipedes, scorpions, tarantulas, and *rattlesnakes*. What's even more amazing and not-giving-a-shit worthy is that even in hunting, roadrunners still decide not to take advantage of their ability to take to the skies and just run down their prey and if the

BACK THE F*CK

BACK THE F*CK UP!

prey doesn't comply, be it tarantula or rattlesnake, the roadrunner will grab the bitch, jump and slam it on the ground until compliance is met, and the roadrunner can start eating.

Hey, but don't look down upon the other species within the cuckoo family that decide to fly. They are devious in their own ways. Many species in the cuckoo family decide that parenthood is for suckas, so instead what they do is find other species of birds that do watch over and take care of their young. They promptly evict them from their nest and then *lay their own eggs in the nest and leave.* The evicted birds soon return to see what the fuck just went on and do nothing about this new adopted egg.

> **These guys are murderers in *their first hours of life.***

"TELL THE CUCKOOS I CAN'T REFUSE THEIR OFFER..."

The fuckery doesn't just end here, though. When the baby cuckoo bird hatches (cuckoo chicks have evolved to hatch faster than most other species of birds), the first thing it does is roll the other non-cuckoo eggs out of the nests and onto the ground multiple feet down. These guys are murderers in *first hours of life.* Being the only chick in the nest, the adoptive parents are forced to take care of their "child" even if in most cases, it ends up becoming much bigger than its "parents." I think the cuckoo family, like the Corleone family, is not a group you would want to mess with ...

BACK THE F*CK UP!

DRINKING TREE SHREWS

Shrews don't really get a good reputation. They don't get the same terrified response people give to rats when they come upon them; neither do they get the longing stares that people give to hamsters and guinea pigs.

Even the acclaimed Brian Jacques' *Redwall* fantasy series has most of them as uneducated (in an universe where rodents are basically people and build castles and towns and wear armor and fight with swords) and tribe-like, speaking in basic tongues. I think we may have found out why—*they are always hammered.*

Well, a specific species of shrew, anyway: the pen-tailed tree shrew. For some reason, scientists decided the interesting thing about these shrews was not that they drank alcohol, but that their tails are somehow pen shaped. Let me assure you, that is not the most interesting thing about them. When I say that the tree shrew drinks alcohol, I don't mean they go to the nearest corner store to purchase a six-pack, which they promptly drink in a lonely alley or something. What they do is drink natural alcohol that can only be found in a plant in Malaysia (where the pen-tailed tree-shrew roam) called the Bertam palm. This plant ferments its nectar to a cool 3.8 percent alcohol content, which is comparable to most human beer.

Oh well! So what if this shrew drinks a bit? Many other animals drink, too, right? Of course. It just happens that those

They are always hammered.

animals drink it as a supplement, whilst the tree shrews drink it *and it alone*. The fermented nectar is its lone sustenance and they spend two hours a day just sipping at it, *every day, 365 days a year*. This is roughly the equivalent of a human drinking 11 glasses of wine a *day, forever*. You can only imagine the kind of parties that these shrews would throw: Everything is covered in puke and random fights starting for no reason, but *BOOOOOZE* ... Hell yeah!

> You can only imagine the kind of parties that these shrews would throw: Everything is covered in puke and random fights starting for no reason.

JACK SPARROW AND HIS RUM HAVE GOT NOTHIN' ON BLUTO BLUTARSKY – NOT WHEN HIS SPIRIT ANIMAL IS THESE GUYS.

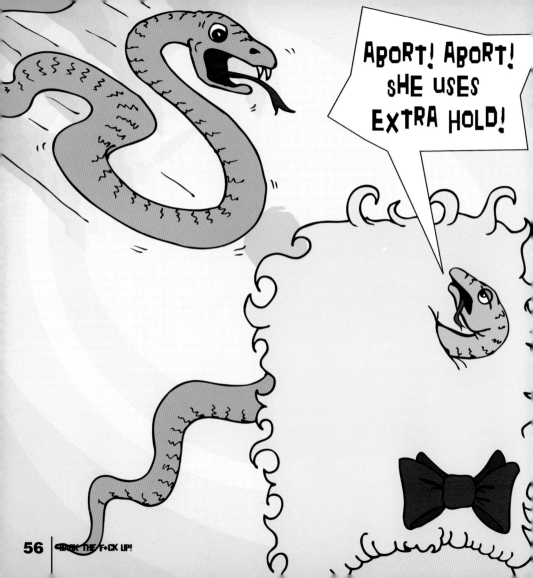

FLYING SNAKES

A snake *that flies*. Do you seriously need more convincing? I suppose you do, since you are still reading. Let's clear something up. The snake doesn't actually fly in the sense that birds fly. They sort of glide, which isn't that much better for us since they can glide up to *780 feet*. And how do they achieve this stupendous feat? By merely *slithering* in the air.

The physics of it all baffles scientists so much that even the *US Department of Defense* has funded a research program just on the flying snake to see if there can be any military applications of this bizarre ability to sort of just slither and glide a long distance.

Luckily, flying snakes aren't particularly dangerous to humans, as their venom is only "mildly dangerous." It goes without saying, though, that if a snake just glided into your hair, you would definitely be shitting your pants. God only knows what will happen if the flying snake decides to start teaching its more dangerous cousins the art of gliding.

> **If a snake just glided into your hair, you would definitely be shitting your pants.**

GIANT AMAZONIAN CENTIPEDES

Fucking terrifying. That is all I have to say. Let's move on. Wait, what? I'm contractually obligated to write a "significant portion" about each animal? Come on, this is a centipede that is more than a *fucking foot long*.

And also they eat bats. Wait, what?

That's right. One day, a bunch of Amazonian centipedes must have met up and decided that they were deserving of a meal that was more than insects and other small, insignificant creatures. What centipedes needed were *bats*. **Of course.** Then a centipede near the back of this hypothetical centipede town hall meeting realized a problem. "But centipedes can't fly!," it shouted. What the centipedes did next, no one could have predicted.

The centipedes climb to the ceilings of bat caves. They then hang from the ceiling with only 10 of their many legs holding them up whilst the rest dangle, waiting for a bat to rush in and get caught. Note that bats are actually bigger than the centipedes by weight and size. The centipede will continue to hang there with bat in its legs until it has finished eating.

They are also venomous, but screw that—they hang from the ceiling and catch things. If you are in a low-ceilinged cave, I don't think a centipede will discriminate between a bat and your *face*.

> **A centipede won't discriminate between a bat and your *face*.**

GOLDEN EAGLES

Golden eagles are eagles. By that logic, they are instantly awesome, because eagles are awesome (except Philadelphia Eagles, screw 'em [that was a joke, please don't kill me, you crazy Philly fans!]). But as far as eagles go, golden eagles are at the top. Being found nearly everywhere in the Northern Hemisphere, it is clear that the golden eagle is able to adapt to many different situations. They can also eat all sorts of things, from the trivial, like marmots, mice, and rabbits, to the less trivial of caribou, deer, swans, and wolves. Also bear cubs. *Fucking bears.*

It isn't, however, what they eat that makes golden eagles so interesting, but *how* they catch it. The golden eagle isn't small, but it isn't a heavyweight. Sure it could probably bring down a fox or wolf by diving

I KIDNAPPED A BEAR. WHAT HAVE *YOU* DONE TODAY?

down from the sky, but caribou and deer? That takes a different kind of badassery. They swoop down to first freak out the caribou or deer. Whilst the caribou or deer is running, the eagle continues to make passes at it to steer the animal to where the eagle wants it: *over a fucking cliff*. Once the said deed has been done, the eagle gets to feast. It's not just helpless deer and caribou that are subject to having the shit scared out of them. Bears get it, too, but golden eagles don't eat them, so the only logical explanation is that it is all for shits and giggles.

Golden eagles are, however, highly partial to bear cubs, and have been well known to snatch them away from their parents, thereby breaking the universal law of don't mess with bears that has been cemented in our minds by the unfinished parable of *Goldilocks and the Three Bears*. Unfinished because it doesn't talk about how after Goldilocks ran away, the three bears chased her down and turned her into minced meat. But don't worry—a golden eagle promptly came by and scared their shit away, whilst abducting Baby Bear. Goldilocks is still dead, though. Apologies for destroying your childhood.

The eagle continues to steer the animal to where the eagle wants it: *over a fucking cliff.*

NOT SO FANTASTIC NOW, EH MR. FOX?

HAIRY FROGS

QUICK! WHO IS THE COOLEST X-MAN? If you just went, "What's an X-Man?," you are probably reading the wrong book. Go and do some research in the comic books section, gramps!

Now if you know what an X-Man is and you said anything other than Wolverine, then you are sorely mistaken. But due to the benevolence of this book and its writer, you are allowed a second chance. Yup! Wolverine is the coolest! And not only because Hugh Jackman is a handsome bloke.

No, it's the fucking claws that come out of his knuckles. Nothing says, "I can beat the shit out of

Breaking its own bones so that they puncture and protrude from its skin...now the frog has a weapon and knows how to use it.

BACK THE F*CK UP

you if you don't run away right now!" than slowly revealing your blades of horror from your knuckles. Believe it or not, there are animals in the wild that try to mimic that badassery.

Like the hairy frog. Yep, the animal in question is a frog, probably the most helpless creature on the planet when it comes to fighting ability. They are smooth, slimy, and have no sharp edges to speak of. They are so harmless, schools are totally fine with letting kids cut them open for "educational" purposes. The hairy frog, however, wasn't going to have any of that shit, but what was a frog supposed to do? I'll tell you. The hairy frog decided that if it didn't have any sharp edges with which to menace others with (like teeth or claws), then it jolly will make one! Or two, or however many it deemed necessary. How? *By breaking its own bones so that they puncture and protrude from its skin.* Specifically the bones in its hind legs. Now the frog has a weapon and it knows how to use it. Stabbing is very much on the agenda for the day. Also, the frogs have hair, but if you didn't already guess that, then, well, you should probably read the name "hairy frog" again.

CORRECTION: MY FROG FRIEND AND I WILL BEAT THE SHIT OUT OF YOU, PERIOD.

Hippos will attack animals just for breathing the same air.

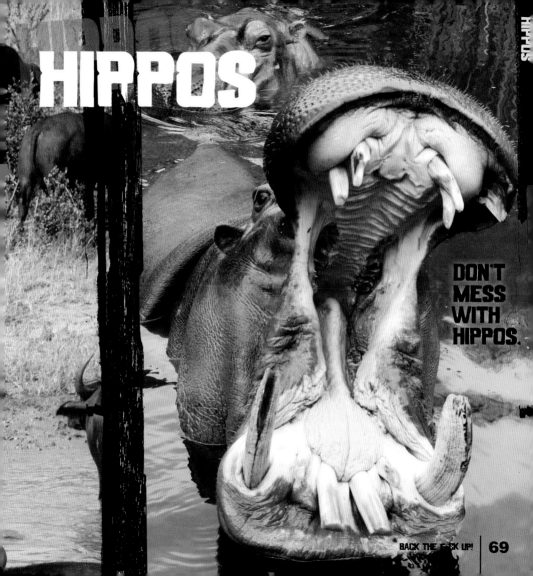

HIPPOS

DON'T
MESS
WITH
HIPPOS.

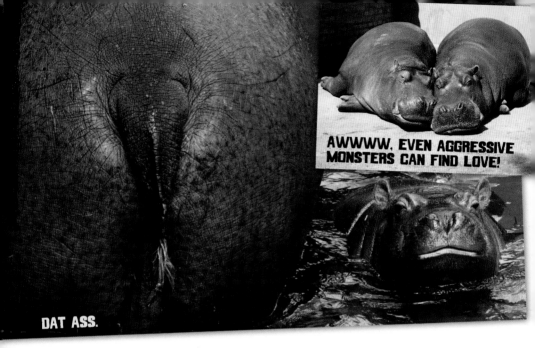

AWWWW, EVEN AGGRESSIVE MONSTERS CAN FIND LOVE!

DAT ASS.

Hippos are cute. Especially when they are young. However, they are also really, really big. But you know this shit already.

What you probably don't know is that whilst in the water, they spin their tails like a little propeller when they poop to fan it out across the water to mark their territory. So essentially, hippos swim in their own feces. But hey, whatever, it's still just animals, maybe they don't know better and have no appreciation for hygiene. Fine. They are also considered by many as the most dangerous animal in Africa.

That's right, *Africa*—the land where elephants, lions, cheetahs, gorillas, and king cobras roam. Of course, they couldn't say the world because Australia has some crazy shit, but the gist of it is: **Don't mess with hippos**. Let's get to know why. Hippos eat such exotic and amazing things like grass, grass, and grass. So, okay, they are herbivores. That, however, doesn't explain why they have *massive teeth* in their mouth that look big and sharp enough to puncture holes in jeeps. It turns out the teeth are more for keeping shit in order. And by shit, I mean crocodiles. That's right—crocodiles are the hippo's bitches. Being too big to be reasonably eaten by crocs, the crocodiles have to put up with being pushed around by hippos, as well as swimming in their shit.

YOU CAN TELL THE HIPPO IS THE DOMINANT ONE IN THIS RELATIONSHIP.

I wish at this point I could just say, "And that's about it! No more stuff about hippos!" Sadly, hippos are just aggressive as fuck. They attack every animal that you can think of if they get in an "unreasonable" distance to them. I quotation mark unreasonable because the distance varies from "you're breathing my air" to "I don't like how you are staring at me from 2 kilometers away, I'm going to run you over now!" Being aggressive to animals therefore translates to aggressive with humans, too. Hippos have been known to attack boats and all manner of human things. Needless to say, hippos have killed many humans.

And just for a final hurrah of shits and giggles, Pablo Escobar, the Colombian drug lord, purchased four hippos in New Orleans and shipped them off to Colombia to live in his compound during the '80s. Escobar is now dead, but when authorities met the hippos, they were at a loss. They had no way to transport four grown hippos back to where they belonged and so they just left them. The hippo herd has now grown and is doing well in its new environment. Being sixteen strong, some have ventured off to new pastures, attacking humans and killing cows, for no fucking reason other than "they were in my field of vision."

BACK THE F*CK UP!

HONEY BADGERS

The honey badger is now Internet famous. Its not-give-a-shittery is completely juxtaposed with its cute name. *Honey* badger. How much cuter can you get? Just with the mention of honey, you imagine the badger would be like a black and white Winnie the Pooh, sitting there sucking on its paws drenched in honey. Awwh! That scene is just darling! Too bad it would never happen, though, because the honey badger is one badass motherfucker.

Let's just start with its name: *The honey badger.* How did a supposedly badass animal get this ludicrously non-badass name? Well, the answer is honey badgers attack beehives and eat ... something from there. For many years, people assumed honey, but it turns out it was actually the larvae; the honey was just an extra little bonus. And let's get this straight. The honey badger roams Africa, so the bees that the honey badger has to deal with are properly Africanized bees, the most aggressive kind that sting like crazy. The honey badger couldn't give half a shit. It gets stung so many times by the bees, which are trying to protect their babies, and it just keeps going on like the Juggernaut. Contrast this to bears in North America who get scared off (after just trying to steal honey) by puny *normal bees.* This, dear reader, is merely the tip of the iceberg.

Whilst being the same size as a smallish dog, it is more aggressive than an attack dog on crack cocaine. Honey badgers have been known to take on lions, leopards, and all sorts of other large African predators. They have also been known to win a lot, too, but not always, because even monkeys fall out of trees sometimes. Also, when hunting, they literally go to the ends of the earth to get what they want.

> **Whilst being the same size as a smallish dog, it is more aggressive than an attack dog on crack cocaine.**

A honey badger has been filmed climbing a really large tree to get at a *king cobra*. It troubled itself to get into an even more troubling situation, since it's not like king cobras are harmless. But the crowning moment of badassery is brought to you by National "We Lie Sometimes" Geographic. A camera crew was following a honey badger known as Kleinman. Kleinman was feeling peckish, as honey badgers are wont to do, and set upon trying to find a snack. Kleinman came across a king cobra and immediately attacked it. Normally, when an animal attacks something as dangerous as a king cobra, they will stop, think, and then run away or know that they have some really amazing strategy that will work because one bite from the cobra and you're pretty much finished. Not Kleinman, though! What is this "stre-ta-gee" that you speak of? Sure, Kleinman had a plan, and that plan was to march right in and clobber and bash the bastard till it was dead and then start eating—so that is what Kleinman did.

Also, honey badgers like to rip people's testicles off.

A few minutes later, you saw Kleinman chewing on the head of the dead king cobra. Sadly, in the fight where Kleinman just straight out clobbered the king cobra, he sustained *multiple bites*. From a king cobra, which is extremely venomous—so venomous that a single bite can kill a human. Kleinman, after just beasting through the large amounts of venom that was coursing through his veins, enough to hypothetically kill two, maybe three, elephants, finally passed out. So there lied the brave, but naïve, Kleinman the badger, may he, and his badassery, rest in peace.

Just fucking kidding. Three hours later, Kleinman woke up, seemingly a-okay and then just kept eating the king cobra as if nothing happened.

Also, honey badgers like to rip people's testicles off. Honey badgers constantly play fight by ripping at *each other's testicles*. It's just a thing; don't breathe too much into it. I'm pretty sure there's a reasonable explanation.

JUST NAPPING IN THE
MIDDLE OF THE PLAINS
ALL VISIBLE AND SHITS
UNGIVEN. FUCK THEM
LIONS AND OTHER
LARGER PREDATORS!

HORNED PACMAN FROGS

The South American horned frog is interestingly named the "Pacman frog," for it has many similarities to Pac-Man. They aren't just the same because of the frog's yellow color and roundness, but also because they both share many behavioral similarities.

BACK THE F*CK UP!

Let's have a quick recap shall we? Pac-Man is a yellow round thing that actively eats everything in his path. On occasion he finds the ability to eat something much bigger than what he would normally eat, also known as ghosts, but he still finds a way to gobble them up with reckless abandon. The frog is a yellow round thing that actively eats nearly everything that gets in its path such as bugs, worms, and other small animals. On occasion, it starts eating much bigger things such as mice, parakeets, and other animals that can be as big as their mouths.

> **The shittery that is not given comes when you find out that Pacman frogs have been known to routinely try to swallow animals much too big for them.**

The shittery that is not given comes when you find out that Pacman frogs have been known to routinely try to swallow animals much too big for them. The thing about the Pacman frog that sets it apart from the rest is that they actually have sharp teeth. These teeth help the frog to grip onto food and swallow it easier. The problem comes when they try to eat food that is too big. They simply just choke to death because the teeth do not allow them to just spit out the food. But even though many members of the species have died from not being able to swallow, they still do it, and continue to die. But I suppose if you're a frog that has the ability to either eat or do nothing, committing suicide through eating is probably the only thing you *can* do.

They are also cannibalistic and have attempted (and have been successful) at eating their mates, even if they are larger than them. And yes, they really do eat rats, mice, and all other kinds of animals. Just search "Pacman frog" on YouTube and you will get hundreds of hits filled with Pacman frogs eating whatever animal the cameraman was able to afford.

IMMORTAL JELLYFISH

STINGERS

Jellyfish, in general, are scary shit. The mere sighting of one near a beach forces the lifeguards on duty to clear the beach. But it's good to know that at the end of the day, many jellyfish succumb to death. Not the immortal jellyfish, though. As its name suggests, the immortal jellyfish cannot die naturally. Once sexually mature, that is, once they've had enough of reproduction and all that jazz associated with adulthood (mid-life crises, tentacle shedding, cheating spouses, and forgone promotion prospects), they can just revert back to their polyp stage at will. Polyp is science's way of saying baby jellyfish.

That's right; the immortal jellyfish is essentially a self-sustaining fountain of youth. And they also *reproduce*. Since none of them die, their numbers just continue to grow, which kind of follows the rising number of jellyfish around the world. Large dense groups of jellyfish have been found all over the world. Scientists at the Smithsonian call it "a silent invasion." But I think it should be called "the apocalypse."

You might think I might be overstating things, but if jellyfish ever figure out how to interbreed between species, there is a species of jellyfish known as the Irukandji, which are more tentacle than jelly. Their tentacles are, on average, about a meter long whilst the actual jelly part of the Irukandji is not much bigger than the tip of a baby's pinkie. As I said, jellyfish are scary shit. Add the fact that they don't actually do anything but just, sort of, flop about and you realize we are afraid of an animal *just for existing*.

Add the fact that they don't actually do anything but just flop about and you realize we are afraid of an animal *just for existing*.

Lots of bitey bitey is probably about to go down.

YOU'RE NOT A SNAKE! I DON'T FEEL LIKE EATING YOU...YET!

KING COBRAS

King cobras are the shit. At least they would be if I didn't fucking hate snakes with reckless disregard for my own safety and well being. As a person who is absolutely terrified of snakes, I think I am perfectly positioned to comment on how terrifying king cobras are. The answer is pants-shittingly. Thank god I've never come across an actual king cobra before because I don't normally, and

BACK THE F*CK UP!

REMEMBER! DON'T DRINK AND PLAY WITH SNAKES!

neither do I plan to, carry a change of pants around everywhere I go.

But king cobras are the real deal. They are so badass, they eat *other snakes* because they clearly share my hatred of them all. In fact, the only time they don't eat snakes is when there just aren't any snakes left to eat and they are starving. Animals in general tend to not confront snakes, let alone hunt them, but the king cobra is too good for these rules.

But really, it's all about the size and dangerousness of it all. King cobras can grow up to 19 feet long and are the largest venomous snake in the world. Their venom is no joke, either. One bite can kill a fully grown person. But really, did you need to know that to be scared?

Turns out king cobras aren't "true" cobras, whatever that's supposed to mean, but the last thing you will ever see is me, or anybody else for that matter, explaining to them how they are only normal snakes that happen to have a hood and not a "real" cobra. It's not like the king is going to understand, but nonetheless, lots of bitey bitey is probably about to go down.

KOMODO DRAGONS

What do you think would be an effective weapon for killing? A gun? A knife? Your fists? In the animal kingdom, many animals have effectively found weapons that feel right with them, be it sniper rifle-like jets of water from archer fish, bone daggers of the hairy frog, or general chimp kung fu. The Komodo dragon looks upon these animal weapons and decides to fuck that noise and be a hipster. It promptly starts a regimen of terrible oral hygiene.

How can terrible oral hygiene be a weapon? What? Is the Komodo dragon going to *breathe* on animals to death, but instead of spewing fire like a normal dragon,

The kill rate of Komodo dragons in the wild is 100 percent. One-hit fatalities all around!

OH GOD.
THE SMELL.
LISTERINE?
ANYONE?

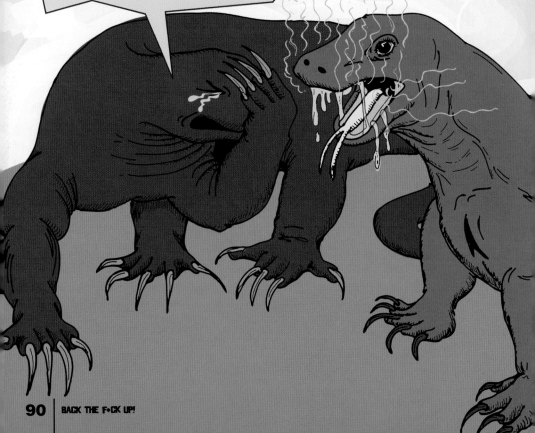

| BACK THE F*CK UP!

spew noxious, disgusting smells? Nope. It's more like biological warfare. Their mouths and saliva are so septic that if a Komodo dragon bites you and you do not get blasted by full-spectrum antibiotics, you will die. Guaranteed. Seeing as how 100 percent of the wild animal population does not have access to such resources, then the kill rate of Komodo dragons in the wild after one bite is *100 percent*. One-hit fatalities all around!

However, a drawback to this amazing weapon that Komodo dragons have acquired makes them the opposite of athletic. When your prey eventually just stops and drops dead because you nibbled on them and all you have to do is casually walk to where the dead carcass is located, there isn't much incentive to go down to the local gym. But don't be fooled; they can still run at 20 kilometers per hour if they feel like it and they have no qualms about attacking you since *it is illegal to kill them by Indonesian law*. Komodo dragons don't give a shit, but mostly because they just don't have to.

> **Komodo dragons don't give a shit, but mostly because they just don't have to.**

OH YES, NOTHING BETTER THAN COW MADE MORE ROTTEN BY OUR VILE ORAL HYGIENE THAT WILL ONLY EXACERBATE THE PROBLEM!

MANAKIN BIRDS

Animals are all about the poontang. Poontang is such a big deal, that they will literally do anything to get some. Stags joust with their heads, walruses impale each other with their tusks, praying mantis get decapitated—it's all for the poontang. Many other animals, however, disagree with this large amount of violence in the bumping-uglies industry and deal with attracting mates with the sacred language of dance. The manakin bird, like many other birds, is one of these animals.

> **Its theory is, to get a girl to like you, you just need more Michael Jackson in that shit.**

Whilst some birds might just jump around on branches and the ground in specific patterns, some are more elaborate and even create their own personal disco where they get down. The manakin bird takes a different approach. More specifically, its theory is, to get a girl to like you, you just need more Michael Jackson in that shit.

Yup, the *moonwalk*. Manakin birds have perfected the moonwalk and use it in an attempt to lure in the chicks. When they do their dance, they are all over that branch, moonwalking backwards, moonwalking forwards, moonwalking sideways left and right. It's amazing. What's even more amazing is that the videos you see on YouTube of it moonwalking are actually slowed down a lot, which is why it looks slightly fake. So not only is it Michael Jackson, it's the fucking Flash.

MANTIS SHRIMP

Mantis shrimp look pretty ordinary. In fact, if you've been to a Chinese seafood restaurant, you've probably eaten them before. So, no big deal, right? *We eat these fuckers.* Turns out we are actually eating the Captain Falcon of the sea. Why? Because these mantis shrimp can really **FALCON PUNCH!**

I want you to try something right now. Go to a swimming pool or something filled with water. Now grab a friend and try to punch him as hard as you can. Unless you're Chuck Norris, your friend probably barely flinched from the non-existent pain that you just exacted on him. Why? Because water slows you down a shit ton. But a Mantis shrimp looks at this physics of it all and goes, "Meh," and

NOW COMES IN ASSASSIN'S CREED COLORS!

> **Mantis shrimp have been known to easily punch through aquarium glass, as well as the thick armor of large crabs, *like it was only Styrofoam*.**

immediately starts punching shit at *50 mph*. That's like being hit by a fucking train *underwater*.

The resulting power is equivalent to 10,000 times the force of gravity, which could probably really fuck up your day if you get hit. In fact, the punch is so fast that it actually *lowers the pressure around the punch,* essentially forming a hadouken which *boils water all around it.* To emphasize how strong these punches are, mantis shrimp have been known to easily punch through aquarium glass, as well as the thick armor of large crabs, *like it was only Styrofoam.*

Then you have their eyes. Whilst puny human eyes are only able to see what we call "visible light," for mantis shrimp, "visible light" includes *ultraviolet, infrared, and polarized light.* For us to see this kind of stuff, we need to build highly sophisticated and expensive machinery. Mantis shrimp are just born with it, *to help them Falcon punch things better.*

THE SIMILARITIES ARE UNCANNY!

BACK THE F*CK UP!

MONGOOSE

Due to Animal Planet and Discovery Channel, you probably know what a mongoose is. Therefore, you probably know that mongoose eat many things that we normally say, "Holy shit, let's run away as fast as we can" to. These animals include, but are not limited to, *scorpions and snakes.* Even the smallest, the common dwarf mongoose, which averages about 7 inches in length, eat these monsters of horror that are usually much larger than the dwarf mongoose themselves.

Sure, dwarf mongoose eat snakes and scorpions. Big whoop ... that's hardly "not giving a shit"; they're just getting sustenance, even if it's only one of the most dangerous ways possible. The thing is, we haven't talked about the Indian mongoose yet. These guys fight fucking *king cobras*, the snake that I just mentioned earlier and of which you should be kind of terrified.

Mongoose aren't heavy-handed like honey badgers, though; they have a certain prowess about them. They use their superior speed and reflexes to

> **These guys fight fucking *king cobras*, of which you should be kind of terrified.**

SIMONE'S BADASS COUSIN, THRICE REMOVED, ON THE MOTHER'S SIDE.

BACK THE F*CK UP!

draw the snake into making multiple missed attacks. It continues to dance around the snake until the snake becomes tired or the mongoose gets bored (we may never know, no cobra has ever lived to answer questions, let alone be able to communicate with researchers), wherein the mongoose will then just lunge out at the snake's head and crush it to death. *One-hit fatality.*

Before you scream, "But they are just hunting them for food right!?!" you should probably know that after some intensive scientific research, it turns out that Indian mongoose don't really have a soft spot for cobra, or any snake for that matter. Yes, they eat the meat sometimes, but prefer to avoid it as food. So really, the Indian mongoose just kills them for the hell of it. It has gotten so bad for cobras, they actually find it necessary when they come across mongoose *to slither away as fast as they can* or at the very least try to scare it away with hissing. Let's just think about that. Cobras that can get up to 18 feet long absolutely fear small mammals at 2 feet long. I'm pretty sure that evolution, and the fact that not many of the latter kind of cobra survive, is the only reason why we aren't hearing about mass cobra genocides. Or maybe nobody cares. Fuck them snakes.

YES, REST DEAR MONGOOSE, YOU'VE EARNED YOUR KEEP WITH THE SNAKE-OCIDE.

OCTOPUS

Octopuses are amazing, although their precognitive abilities are highly debatable, even if Paul the octopus was able to guess the eventual winners of the majority of the 2010 FIFA World Cup. Octopuses still have lots of badassery leftover, though, which is exhibited by the mimic octopus.

The mimic octopus is the master of disguises when it comes to animals. Sure, caterpillars can imitate ant larvae or queens, but they look nothing alike. Mimic octopuses, on the other hand, can make themselves look exactly like sea snakes and flatfish or even the *mantis shrimp*. You will never know what you truly are looking at until the octopus decides to spray you with ink and make a run for it.

Octopuses, in general, are flexible as hell due to the fact that they are invertebrates. A large octopus can squeeze its own body through a bottle if it really wants to. What is amazing is their ability to learn. Sure, learning, great. Many animals can learn, like, for example, the whales! Well, yeah, orcas learn because they actually have parents to teach them things, but not octopuses. The octopus never knows its parents and thus never really needs to learn things, as much as instinctively do things. Yet, *no.* Octopuses are given amazing learning abilities in the form of exceptional long- and short-term memory. They have been known to break out of aquariums to search for food and individual octopus have been known to *climb onto fishing boats, open holds, and eat the crabs found inside*.

Add the fact that octopuses have shown the ability to survive out of water for significant amounts of time and you have a monster capable of genocide.

They are the only invertebrate known to actually use tools. They have even been known to *build shelters for themselves* out of manipulated coconut shells. Let's not even go into the fact that octopuses

NOPE.
WASHING
MY HANDS
ISN'T
WORTH
THIS SHIT!

are able to *play* and seem to enjoy themselves in an activity that doesn't involve dicking about with other animals and killing them.

It's not all happiness and joy, though. When going to Australia, beware of the blue-ringed octopus. The venom found in one bite by a blue-ringed octopus can kill 26 individual people. Add the fact that octopuses have shown the ability to survive out of water for significant amounts of time and you have a monster capable of genocide. Thanks a fuckload, *Australia*.

SHELL SHOCK! THIS CRAFTY LITTLE OCTOPUS HAS BUILT ITSELF A HIDING PLACE BETWEEN ONE NUT SHELL AND ONE CLAM SHELL.

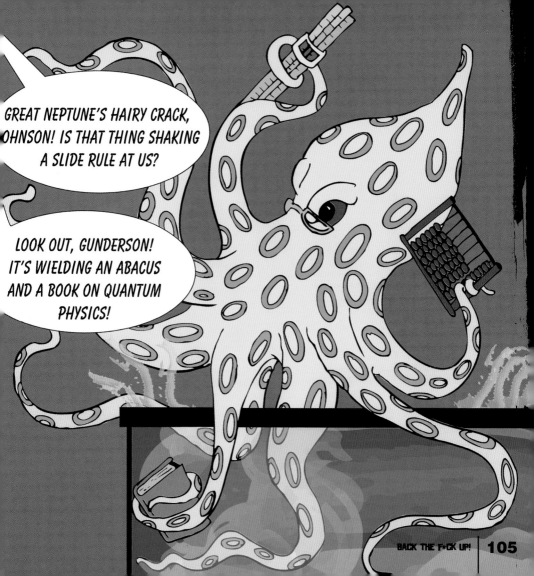

| BACK THE F*CK UP!

ORCAS

Orcas are so cool! Remember going to Sea World and watching them jump through hoops and splashing everybody? Everybody loves them! It just so happens that we forget that the more common name for them is *killer* whales. Where did this even come from? Look at them eat those sardines! Well, it's quite simple really—the Latin name for orcas is Orcinus orca, which roughly translates to "beings that belong to the kingdom of the dead." Spanish sailors called them balena asesina, which roughly translates to "whale assassin." Although they don't go around in white hoods stabbing people with wrist knives (they don't have wrists), they do kill many things.

> **The orca is called the killer whale. And it is well deserved, because if it lives and exists, the orca will find a way to kill it.**

And if you think about it for a second, great white sharks aren't called "killer" sharks. Giant squid aren't called "killer" squid. Yet, the orca is called the killer whale. And it is well deserved, because if it lives and exists, the orca will find a way to kill it. For example, great white sharks are a common snack for orcas and it isn't even a fair fight. If you were hoping for an epic duel to the death, I apologize, but orcas merely use their intellect and just flip sharks upside down, thereby kicking in the shark's tonic immobility, and the orca is free to feast in peace and relative safety. An orca's diet varies depending on where they live, for they may live in waters where the only thing of any value to eat is salmon, but because the orca can be found in every ocean, there isn't really anything that they don't eat.

Not even the largest fish in the world, the whale shark, is safe; it merely takes two orcas to kill it quickly. Sperm whales? Easy pickings. Blue whales? *The largest living animal ever to grace its presence on Earth?* Simpler than counting to three. To even think about making it difficult for orcas, you're going to have to not be in the

> **'Safe' isn't a word that exists if what you're trying to stay away from are orcas.**

ocean. Seals and sea lions usually use the fact that they can waddle around on land as an advantage to stay safe from killer whales. Just kidding! "Safe" isn't a word that exists if what you're trying to stay away from are orcas. Orcas have perfected the ability to partially beach themselves and grab seals, penguins, and all other kinds of land-dwelling beasts. They've even been known to eat reindeer and moose, just because they can. It's not just about eating, though; killer whales have been known to kill seals and porpoises *just for laughs*.

It would probably be okay to know that killer whales are effective killing machines. They clearly earn their names. I mean, they are wild animals, what are you going to do? An animal, at the end of the day, is a fucking animal. It's not like you expect it to come over for tea and crumpets and have it point out its non-existent pinky whilst holding the tea cup! It just so happens that killer whales are also highly intelligent. They frequently learn new tricks of the trade, the trade being killing, from each other. For example, a captive killer whale (so the nice kind) figured out that it could eat seagulls and other birds if it just *regurgitated a bit of fish onto the water*. The four other captive orcas quickly followed suit. An average middle schooler wouldn't come up with that solution! The famous beaching trick is taught from mother to calf. They have even been known to catch seals *and then release them* so that the younger whales can practice the technique on *weakened opponents*.

But don't let all of this killing fool you—they can be pretty friendly and playful, too! Sometimes, when a person is trying to reach for something in the water, the killer whale will actually *move it away from the person* playfully. One time, some researcher thought it would be a good idea to throw a fucking snowball at a killer whale. The killer whale, not being a party pooper, returned the favor and lobbed a *fucking large chuck of ice back at the researcher*. But it's probably good to know that of all the carnivorous animals in this book, orcas are the only ones that don't really eat humans. At least not on a regular basis ...

SOON...ONLY THE
FREE FISH WILL
KEEP YOU SAFE!

BACK THE F*CK UP!

PISTOL SHRIMP

So you've met the mantis shrimp. Surely the hadoukening, **FALCON PUNCH!** master is the most badass of the shrimp world! Well, then you haven't met the fastest slinger of the deep blue seas: the pistol shrimp. Whilst mantis shrimp can grow up to nearly a foot long, pistol shrimp are barely longer than a quarter is wide, but don't let size deceive you.

Although the pistol shrimp don't carry around .45s like their name suggests, they do have one massively over-sized claw on one arm. What is this claw for you ask? Punching? *RIPPING HOLES IN THE SPACE TIME CONTINUUM?!?* Nope, just snapping.

At least, that's what scientists call what can only be described as a *"literal fucking sonic rifle."* Remember the 50 mph hadouken from the mantis shrimp? The pistol shrimp can snap its claw at *60 mph.* This causes the pressure to decrease significantly and create cavitation, which boils the water instantly. Except the water isn't just boiling, *but at 4,700 degrees Celsius*, which in comparison to the Sun at 5500 degrees, is quite a big deal.

This is sort of like archer fish meets mantis shrimp. The jets of superheated water can knock anything unconscious, leaving the pistol shrimp to live in peace. In a head-to-head fight between the pistol shrimp and mantis shrimp, there is only

The fastest slinger of the deep blue seas ... at least, that's what scientists call what can only be described as a 'literal fucking sonic rifle.'

No one is ever going to make masturbation jokes about its excessively large right arm ever again!

one possible outcome. The mantis shrimp actually has to physically hit the pistol shrimp, whilst the pistol shrimp can just shoot it from afar. Also, the pistol shrimp is faster. Pistol shrimp win. No one is ever going to make masturbation jokes about its excessively large right arm ever again!

Even Mother Nature realized that she overpowered the pistol shrimp too much, so in order to compensate, gave it such shitty near-sightedness that it is no longer really viable for pistol shrimp to take over the world, unless they invent corrective glasses, then all bets are off.

SOME PISTOL SHRIMP HAVE A SYMBIOTIC RELATIONSHIP WITH GOBY FISH. THE GOBY LOOKS OUT FOR DANGER AND THE SHRIMP BEATS UP ANY INTRUDERS WITH ITS POPEYE-ESQUE ARM.

PLATYPUS

The platypus is an animal that shits all over evolution. With the tail of a beaver, beak of a duck, egg-laying ability of non-mammalians, feet of otters, and the ability to create venom (another thing that mammals don't usually do unless they have evil underground lairs), platypuses were originally deemed hoaxes by European scientists.

> **The platypus is an animal that shits all over evolution. It's like Mother Nature just had a ton of spare parts left for Australia and instead of creating a few more different species of animals, she decided, 'You know what would be hilarious ... ?'**

Why should it not surprise us that platypus are from Australia? Oh right, because Australia is just filled with crazy shit like that.

Then there is another ability that platypuses can perform that is just completely atypical from normal mammalian behavior. They can detect *magnetic fields generated by living organisms*. It's like Mother Nature just had a ton of spare parts left for Australia and instead of creating a few more different species of animals, she decided, "You know what would be hilarious? Not just the duck bill, and the outrageous cuteness, but the fact that it has barbs on its hind legs that *can inject dangerous venom into whatever it wants to.*"

That's right—although the venom is unlikely to be able to kill you, it could most definitely cripple you. But at least platypuses are outrageously adorable!

| BACK THE F*CK UP!

NO! DON'T LOOK AT ME!
MY FUR COAT IS DIRTY!

POLAR BEARS

Awwwh! Polar bears! Don't we just all love polar bears? They seem so big and white and furry and cuddly! Okay, you can now let go of your polar bear plushies. As you know, in the same way that a teddy bear isn't a good representation of what a normal bear is like, neither is a plushie even remotely similar to the actual thing, and other than the whiteness, I think we can all agree on that.

> **One second you get a cute fluffy and blubbery seal. Add a polar bear to the equation and the next second you get some snow covered with blood stains and possibly some fur. _Cuteness means nothing to polar bears._**

Polar bears have been getting a lot of love recently. With this whole climate change thing, polar bears have essentially become the mascots of saving the planet in the same way that pandas are all about saving the animals (we just love our bears for some reason). Love truly is blind. We fail to forget that polar bears are the largest carnivorous animals on the _entire planet_. Not only that, but they consistently kill seal, probably the cutest animal on the planet. One second you get a cute fluffy and blubbery seal. Add a polar bear to the equation and the next second you get some snow covered with blood stains and possibly some fur. _Cuteness means nothing to polar bears._ But that's fine, we get it, adorableness doesn't feed the family. A bear's gotta eat.

OH...HI?
FML.

The polar bear's sense of smell is exceptional. Not only are they able to smell their prey from a whole mile away, they can smell them through three whole feet of _solid ice and snow_. They are also surprisingly fantastic swimmers, with bears quite commonly found 200 miles away from the coast. Add the fact that they can run at 25 miles per hour and you have an extremely solid killing machine.

It's not just helpless seals, though; walruses and their three-feet-long ivory tusks are formidable weapons, but even they fall victim to polar bears,

OH ... WOW,
POLAR BEARS
ARE KINDA CUTE!

as do *fucking whales*. Polar bears are also the only animal on Earth known to actively hunt humans. Whereas brown bears only severely maul humans and then run away, when a polar bear attacks, it means business. Polar bears have been known to kill and eat humans and the only reason we don't hear about mass killings is because not many humans actually live in the Arctic. And the scary thing is, *they are stealth hunters.* They will totally Sam Fisher your ass. You won't know that you're even being hunted ... until it's too late.

Polar bears are pretty hygienic, too. Like a professional assassin, after every kill/meals, it's all the same to polar bears, they clean themselves in snow and water. Well, at least their cubs are cute! Just don't get too close—the mom is probably already behind you.

> **Polar bears are also the only animal on Earth that have been known to actively hunt humans ... And the scary thing is, *they are stealth hunters*. They will totally Sam Fisher your ass.**

BACK THE F*CK UP!

RABBITS

Rabbits! Everybody loves bunny wabbits! Bugs Bunny for god's sake! And, really, you shouldn't stop loving them! They are so cute and cuddly and fuzzy and oh so very huggable! Don't worry, rabbits don't have a secret dark side—unless you consider boning at levels that border on severe sex addiction a "dark side."

When people say, "fucking like bunnies," they have no idea what they are talking about. The rates at which rabbits procreate are unreal. Can you guess what the most damaging pest is in Australia,

Rabbits don't have a secret dark side—unless you consider boning at levels that border on severe sex addiction a 'dark side.'

WHEN THE MOON HITS YOUR EYE LIKE A BIG-A PIZZA PIE, THAT'S AMORE!

BACK THE F-CK UP!

the international land of horror? Yup. *Rabbits.* Not cane toads, not any other fucking terrifying animal that lives in Australia. Rabbits. Why? Just because of how many of them there are.

It all started when a man named Thomas Austin moved to Australia. Being a rich Englishman, all that was on his mind was what he could shoot with a gun. Seeing no rabbits around the plains of Australia, the solution dawned upon him. He needed to get *rabbits shipped over to Australia.* Fine, it's not like there weren't perfectly good kangaroos and whatnot to shoot at. Twelve rabbits were sent over and he promptly had his fun, or at least he would have if he had found them.

Once the rabbits were let out, they blended so well into the environment (and Austin was such a terrible shot) that they just weren't killed. Well whoop-dee-fucking-doo. Twelve rabbits. This is *Australia* we're talking about, those rabbits wouldn't last a week. Many years on and now you have 15 times more rabbits than there are people in Australia. That's over 300 million rabbits. Twelve to *300,000,000.*

Rabbits are such a problem that they are one of the main causes for why you aren't allowed to bring anything remotely biological into Australia. What exact problems are we talking about? *Rabbits are the number one cause for animal extinctions in Australia.* But the rabbits don't know any better. They're just chewing on carrots and boning to their heart's content. They don't know that all their resources gobbling is fucking over native species!

They don't know that all their resources gobbling is fucking over native species!

YES, THE WHITE FLUFFINESS IS ALL A FACADE–BENEATH IT IS AN ORANGE FUZZINESS!!

RED PANDAS

Contrary to what the name suggests, red pandas are not normal pandas that are red. They aren't even bears! They do come from China, though, which just confuses the shit out of everything. That doesn't mean they aren't cute, though. If you've never seen one before, imagine the cutest fox cub you've ever seen. Now give it puppy and kitten features. Now dunk the bastard in red paint and voila! Red panda! It's so wuvly and *CUTE*! At this point, you're probably thinking, "Oh here it goes again, so what ... Does this animal rip people's faces off? No, wait! Does it kill pandas? Is that why they are called red pandas because they are *constantly covered by panda blood?!?!*"

No. The story behind red pandas is that they are really friendly! Yay! A little *too friendly.* How can you be too friendly? Keep in mind these are legitimate wild creatures. They have never lived with humans before, but put a human and some red pandas in a room and they will become extremely *fast friends.* Red pandas are so playful and friendly toward humans, it borders on no shit given *toward their own safety.* And it's not like they are hulking massive leviathans, capable of bringing pain in harder than Mr. T. They are merely the size of an average domestic cat.

They want to be *our friends*, no matter how many guns we point at them for their fur.

Everything says that these animals should avoid humans, but they just make every indication that they want to be *our friends*, no matter how many guns we point at them for their fur. We have got to stop the killing of them so that we can all have one to be our best friend!

NO MORE PWAY
TODAY ... KTHXBAI!

SNAKEHEAD FISH

The snakehead fish must be another amalgamation of parts from Mother Nature's Halloween box that she thought would be fun to play around with. It's the only possibility. As the name suggests, the snakehead fish has a head that highly resembles that of a snake. And it's not like they're small or something. Snakehead fish have been known to be in excess of *one meter* (more than three feet). Although they are farmed to a certain extent in some Asian countries, it's probably less about food, as it is cultivating horrors.

They are adaptable and have taken to invading places that they would normally not belong to, like mainland USA, where they are just appearing all over the place from California to Virginia. They wreak havoc on their new homes since they are extremely voracious eaters, eating anything from small insects to frogs, to small fish, large fish ... and rats, birds, and creatures that don't live in the water. Remember the archer fish and how it gets past the barrier known as air by shooting jets of water at things? Well, the snakehead fish has a secret. That secret is that it looks at this protective barrier that we humans like to call "not water" and thinks "big fucking deal" and slithers out of the water and starts *breathing air*.

Snakehead fish have evolved basic lungs, which mean they can breathe air for a significant amount of time. And it's not like they are Magikarp and only know how to splash and flop about on land. They can *slither around like snakes*. When a water source has dried out, they have been known to travel four days or up to a quarter of

We are no longer safe from menaces of the water. God help us all.

a mile to another body of water, all the while chomping on shit in their path that gets too close to their ugly-ass snake head. We are no longer safe from menaces of the water. God help us all.

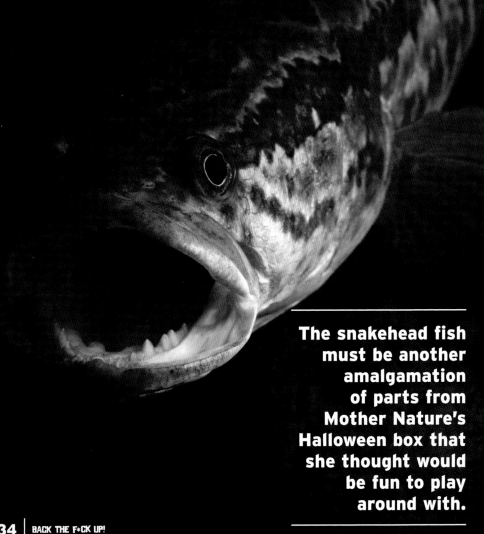

The snakehead fish must be another amalgamation of parts from Mother Nature's Halloween box that she thought would be fun to play around with.

Spotted hyenas are the Spartans of the animal kingdom.

SPOTTED HYENAS

When you think of hyenas, what comes to mind? The pathetic *Lion King* hyenas that eat scraps, but eventually usurp the social structure of the Savannah to become their own leaders through revolution?!? Or maybe you just know them as simple scavengers, eating what lions and other big predators leave behind.

PLEASE! THE LION KING IS A TERRIBLE REPRESENTATION OF THE SOCIO-DEMOGRAPHICAL RELATIONSHIPS THAT OCCUR INTER-SPECIES IN THE SERENGETTI.

BACK THE F*CK UP!

That shit is wrong. Spotted hyenas are arguably the most dominant predator in Africa, with the highest number of kills on the plains over the cheetah, lion, or whatever! And they aren't messy like lions, leaving bones and whatnot all over the place. Hyenas eat the *whole animal.* Flesh, *teeth, and bones.* In fact, the only thing they don't touch is hair, because they aren't fucking cats and they don't do hairballs.

Also, lions and even *hippos* are quite commonly kicked about by hyenas, regardless of the fact that these animals outweigh them multiple times over. The continued existence of the spotted hyenas is surprising most of all, though, because of their reproductive system. When birthed, cubs have to come out of a narrow tube in the mother's clitoris, which kind of looks like a penis. Male and female readers can just imagine how extremely excruciating that is. It doesn't help that the cubs have the largest baby-to-mother weight ratio of carnivorous animals.

But when born, they come out pretty much ready for fighting. By 10 days, they can run at considerable speeds and within months they are already doing adult behavior, like marking their territory. Spotted hyenas are the Spartans of the animal kingdom. There is no such thing as a wimpy hyena.

OM-
NOM-
NOM-
NOM-
NOM!

SQUIRRELS

Too bad behind this veneer of cute and cuddly innocence lives one of the most terrifying animals in the world.

Oh, the squirrel! How adorable it is! Climbing trees and eating nuts! You just want to pick one up, name it Swirly, and be best friends forever and ever! Too bad behind this veneer of cute and cuddly innocence lives one of the most terrifying animals in the world.

Yup, squirrels are terrifying beasts. Did you seriously think all they do is collect acorns for the winter? Whilst you aren't looking, they are thinking of how they can fuck you up. Seriously. There are so many cases of squirrels attacking people, a book could probably be written about it, but the crazier stories of squirrel attacks include one attacking a nurse and promptly *knocking her out*. The attack was so sudden and vicious that from then on, it became hospital policy that no person is out and about *alone and without an umbrella in hand to fend off squirrels*. Then there was the time a squirrel attacked an elementary school, injuring eleven adults and three children. The list just goes on and on.

Maybe squirrels aren't afraid of humans because they are so used to us feeding them and in that sense, we are kind of their bitches. That would be a reasonable explanation, if it wasn't for the fact that they aren't afraid of much larger animals like *deer, large dogs, and snakes*. They have been reported to have attacked all sorts of animals. Probably the most harrowing story is from Russia, where a group of squirrels ganged up on a large stray dog. The dog was killed in *seconds*. When humans approached, only then did the squirrels bolt away, *with dog meat in their mouths*.

Squirrels aren't just aggressive—they have the abilities to pull off crazy things.

Whilst you aren't looking, they are thinking of how they can fuck you up.

It isn't enough to say that squirrels are extremely nimble little critters because we all know that shit. Seeing them climb trees and whatever crazy bullshit squirrels do with such ease, it's clearly apparent to us all that they have the agility and nimbleness of hyperactive acrobats. However, it turns out they aren't just brainless creatures, using their naturally agile bodies. They are able to figure out and climb through convoluted man-made obstacle courses that the majority of *Total Wipeout* contestants would completely fail at, and not just because these obstacle courses are squirrel-sized.

How do we know this? Because of science— specifically, scientists trying to gauge the intelligence of squirrels. Needless to say, squirrels outperformed the scientists' expectations. The ability to learn whole obstacle courses quickly emphasizes the fact that their capacity to learn and solve puzzles is extremely high. And it isn't like these obstacles are a lot of crawling around through some tunnels and climbing up some poles or something trivial like that. They actually make good use of trolleys, running across rollers and all manner of pretty complicated mechanical things that squirrels have probably never come across in their life.

And they don't just show their intellectual capabilities on man-made obstacle courses, either. In the wild, they have also been known to outsmart *snakes,* an animal that *isn't normally considered as retarded*. In order to prevent themselves from getting eaten—they're still squirrels after all—they

YO! WADDUP, PLAYA?

Squirrels have been well known to light themselves on fire and kamikaze into things, like cars, and *making them explode*.

NEXT
UTENSILS
TO LEARN:
KNIVES!

have been known to chew up rattlesnake skin that had been shed, and smear it all over their bodies in order to fool the snakes into thinking that they are one of them. This isn't John "Hannibal" Smith smart, where squirrels think of some elaborate plan with explosions to distract the snake whilst they run away or something. No, they are more Hannibal Lecter ingenious, where they chew the flesh of their enemies and smear it upon themselves because, *fuck all*. They are also able to assess how dangerous a snake is, just by the sound of the *rattle,* because they can. Now they are just showing off!

Sorry, did I say squirrels don't create explosions? What I meant was, squirrels don't cause explosions *sometimes*. Squirrels have been well documented as causing *massive power outages*. And we aren't talking about a random house in some obscure neighborhood. We're talking about whole US Army bases, whole towns, and once, even *Hollywood*, by fucking with the wiring. But what are they doing with the wiring? Apparently, *they are setting shit on fire.* Cases of squirrel-induced arson have skyrocketed in recent years. They have been known to set fire to large acreages of hills, houses of important people, and *elementary schools.* These are just the confirmed cases. Scientists say that they are merely starting fires in order to kill plants in certain areas that don't create enough nuts for them to eat, as opposed to the more fire-resistant plants of the nut-producing variety. That would be all well and good, but it doesn't explain why squirrels have been well known to light themselves on fire and kamikaze into things that are human, like cars, and *making them explode.* Clearly, they want us all dead so they can take our food. *We have to stop giving them peanuts before its too late!*

BACK THE F*CK UP!

SWANS

Swans are elegant creatures. How can they not be? They look absolutely fantastical—purely snow white and with long necks. They are even one of the only animals in the animal kingdom that mate for life, which is sort of the animal equivalent of marriage. If not the kings and queens of the animal kingdom, they are definitely within the animalian aristocracy—a noble of sorts. But like many nobles of old, swans sneer and look down upon lower species—for example, us. They show this disdain with nothing but pure aggression.

Get too close and the swan will go completely apeshit and start biting you and *won't stop till you're dead.*

Sure, you've probably seen swans from afar and just sat there in the park for hours, watching them gracefully glide from lake shore to lake shore. Little did you know the swan was eyeballing you, and everything else in its line of sight. Get too close and the swan will go completely apeshit and start biting you and *won't stop till you're dead*. The fact that they won't stop is underlined by the fact that the only way to protect yourself from a swan attack is by *grabbing it by the neck and throwing it as far as you possibly can and then running away as fast as your legs will allow.

Swans are no joke. Rowing events and practices have been forced to cancel at the mere existence of a swan anywhere near where the boats were going to go. That's large groups of large burly men, dual-wielding paddles, being frightened off like little girls by swans. This certainly gives you food for thought the next time you show up at the park and are considering whether you should throw breadcrumbs for the swans to eat. They might take offense that you, a lowly non-swan, is offering them food or that you might be trying to poison them. When that happens, all you will end up seeing is white—literally.

THIS BEAUTIFUL PHOTO
WAS FOUND ON A SLIGHTLY
BLOODIED CAMERA THAT
WASHED UP ASHORE...

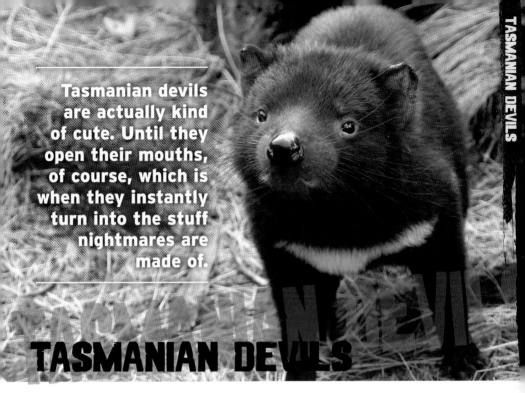

Tasmanian devils are actually kind of cute. Until they open their mouths, of course, which is when they instantly turn into the stuff nightmares are made of.

TASMANIAN DEVILS

The Tasmanian devil has been perpetuated in popular culture by Warner Brothers as the crazy tornado-animal known as Taz. Being a cartoon, Taz gets up to all sorts of mischief like speaking in a gibberish tongue and destroying things. But this can't possibly be what actual Tasmanian devils are like right?

Well, in terms of looks, Taz is a bit off; he walks on his hind-legs and is brown. Tasmanian devils are more like little black bears, and they are actually kind of cute. Until they open their mouths, of course, which is when they instantly turn into the stuff nightmares are made of. Their jaws open up so wide, you'd probably

BACK THE F*CK UP!

forget that their face is anything other than mouth. Then comes the strength of their bite. This beast, the size of a small dog, has the most powerful bite force-to-weight ratio of any mammal. The Tasmanian devil uses this powerful bite to good use by being known to bite through things like skin, bones, and fucking *metal*. That's right. Tasmanian

But let's just say that again: *they bite through metal*.

devils have been known to bite through metal traps for a multitude of reasons such as freeing themselves, or possible meals, from them. But let's just say that again: *they bite through metal*.

It's not all just about the biting, though. The Tasmanian devil is an extreme glutton and hunts all sorts of animals, most of which are bigger than itself, like wombats and kangaroos. What's even more amazing is that when they tuck in, they eat *everything*. Hair? Yep. Bones? Uh-huh! Shoes? Yessiree! Wait, what? Yup. Tasmanian devils are opportunistic. They have been known to eat all sorts of things that no sane animal would consider food such as pencils, pet collars and tags, plastic, jeans, and even completely intact spines of the echidna (a hedgehog-like animal native to Australia). Somehow, the devils see the equivalent of carpet tacks and think to themselves, "What a tasty looking snack!"

It's not just what they eat, though, it's how much. They have been known to eat from 5 percent of their bodyweight to a whopping *40 percent*! That's like an average man eating 145 Big Macs in *one sitting*. If there's food, by god, they will eat that

food up like they have been starving for days! After it's finished its meal, so when it's so bloated it could burst, the Tasmanian devil will just lie down where it is, regardless of how open and dangerous the surroundings are, and just nap. *Nap*. And not another shit will be given by the Tasmanian devil this day.

WOLVERINES

Quick! Who is your favorite X-Man? Feeling a bit of déjà-vu? You should, because you should know that the correct answer is Wolverine. Wolverine the comic book character is a badass, through and through. He isn't afraid of anything and everything is afraid of him. He essentially feels no pain and will fight anything no matter what the odds. Funny thing is that same description can also be given to the animal.

> **One of its favorite ways to kill its prey is by climbing onto the top of tall rocks or tree stumps and then jumping onto the back of unsuspecting prey, like a surprise piggy-back ride gone wrong.**

Although lacking massive retractable claws made of adamantium, the wolverine still has its moments of badassery. It can be found anywhere in the northern tundra, from Russia to Canada, to some parts of the western USA. Wolverines are essentially dog-sized weasels, but don't let that fact make you think that it is a wimp. It has a reputation for killing prey many times its size. Despite its name, it has no relations to the wolf, but it can, however, be equally as cunning. One of its favorite ways to kill its prey is by climbing onto the top of tall rocks or tree stumps and then jumping onto the back of passing, unsuspecting prey, breaking their backs and severing organs in the process, like a surprise piggy-back ride gone wrong. Wolverines attack and eat anything from berries, small rodents, Arctic foxes, musk ox, deer, and bears. Wait ... Hold up ... What?

Yep, no kidding. Wolverines stalk, fight, and periodically eat bears. Wolverines are indiscriminate when it comes to what they fight with, and constantly fight off packs of wolves, black bears, and polar bears for food. These are killing machines we are talking about—killing machines that are multiple times bigger than the gutsy wolverine.

Another name for wolverines is gulo gulo, which roughly translates in Latin to glutton. However, unlike the Tasmanian devils, they don't actually eat more than they need to. Once they have had their fill, they just simply take a *big steamy piss* onto the carcass before burying it to eat later—so, they are essentially eating their own urine-marinated, specially mummified meat. Yummy.

Just to reiterate again: Wolverines *eat bears*. I don't think I can emphasize that enough. **Bears.**

COME SIT WITH ME SO I CAN JUST. UM … ENJOY YOUR PRESENCE … IN MY MOUTH.

OH GOD, IT
SEES US!!!

IMAGE CREDITS

Illustrations on P. 13, 16, 21, 24-25, 27, 30, 36, 39, 46, 50, 54, 56, 58, 64, 66, 72-73, 76, 80, 82, 86, 90, 97, 100, 105, 109, 112, 117, 121, 126, 130, 135, 138, 142, 148, 152, and 156 are by Stacey Leigh Brooks, author of *Creepy-Ass Dolls* and *Diary of a Creepy-Ass Doll.*

Century Fox; P. 68, hippo chasing African cape buffalo: Mark O'Flaherty/Shutterstock; P. 69, hippos: Timothy Craig Lubcke/
Shutterstock; P. 70, baby hippo and mom: Jiri Cvrk/Shutterstock, hippo couple: kajakiki/Shutterstock; P. 71, still from *Fantasia*:
Walt Disney Productions/Heritage Auctions; P. 74, honey badger sitting in a hole: Jag_cz/Shutterstock; P. 78, the fearless
honey badger taking a time out: Matt Gibson/Shutterstock; P. 79, horned pacman frog: Audrey Snider-Bell/Shutterstock;
P. 81, Pac-Man: Namco Ltd.; P. 83, warning sign for dangerous marine stingers or jellyfish in Australia: Johan Larson/
Shutterstock; P. 84, king cobra in northern India: Sam DCruz/Shutterstock; P. 85, king cobra: Heiko Kiera/Shutterstock; P.
87, snake charmers in India: Angelo Giampiccolo/Shutterstock, King Cobra beer: Anheuser-Busch; P. 88, Komodo dragon:
beltsazar/Shutterstock; P. 89, top photo: Komodo dragon: David Evison/Shutterstock; bottom photo: a pair of Komodo
dragons running surprisingly fast toward prey on Komodo Island: Pius Lee/Shutterstock; P. 91, Komodo dragons eating a wild
buffalo, Rinca Island, Indonesia: kkaplin/Shutterstock; P. 94, Underwater macro image of a peacock mantis shrimp in Mabul,
Malaysia: Beverly Speed/Shutterstock; P. 95, mantis shrimp: xjbxjhxm123/Shutterstock; P. 96, Captain Falcon: Nintendo; P. 98,
mongoose: Eric Gevaert/Shutterstock; P. 99, mongoose standing up: Alan Jeffery/Shutterstock; P. 101, banded mongoose:
Jiri Haureljuk/Shutterstock; P. 103, octopus arm coming out of a bathtub faucet: W. Scott/Shutterstock, scary giant octopus:
tepic/Shutterstock; P. 104, octopus traveling with shells: Nick Hobgood/Wikimedia Commons; P. 106, orca jumping out of
the water: Christian Musat/Shutterstock; P. 110, orca with mouth open, looking for food: Karina Wallton/Shutterstock; P. 114,
pistol shrimp and gobi fish: Steve Childs/Wikimedia Commons; P. 115, elusive platypus: Susan Flashman/Shutterstock; P.
116, swimming platypus: Stefan Kraft/Wikimedia Commons; P. 118, yawning polar bear: Bernd Schmidt/Shutterstock; P. 119,
polar bear peek-a-boo: Rene Kohut/Shutterstock; P. 120, polar bears and seal: Michel Loiselle/Shutterstock; P. 122, polar
bear sticking out tongue: Bernhard Richter/Shutterstock; polar bear cub having a rest on his mom's back: Sergey Skleznev/
Shutterstock; polar bear sleeping: poutnik/Shutterstock; P. 123, polar bears fighting: Uryadnikov Sergey/Shutterstock; P. 124,
young rabbit in the grass: Ervin Monn/Shutterstock; P. 125, rabbit couple eating leaf: camelia/Shutterstock; P. 127, hare:
red-feniks/Shutterstock; P. 129, waving red panda: Nick Biemans/Shutterstock; P. 131, red panda sleeping on tree branch:
Reinhold Folger/Shutterstock; P. 132, underwater view of a spotted (cobra) snakehead fish: EcoPrint/Shutterstock; P. 133 and
P. 134, blotched snakehead fish: FormosanFish/Shutterstock; P. 136, hyena family: Sam DCruz/Shutterstock; P. 137, hyena:
poeticpenguin/Shutterstock; P. 139, hyena eating ribs: Albie Venter/Shutterstock; P. 141, squirrel with tongue sticking out:
Patrick Power/Shutterstock; P. 143, red squirrel posing at the park: MrTwister/Shutterstock; P. 144, squirrel drinking from straw:
R Gombarik/Shutterstock; P. 145, squirrel eating a peanut: Bruce MacQueen/Shutterstock; P.146 and P. 149, swans: Vaclav
Volrab/Shutterstock; P. 150, Tasmanian devil opening wide: Ewan Chesser/Shutterstock; P. 151, Tasmanian devil looking cute
and innocent: Ralph Loesche/Shutterstock; P. 153, Tasmanian devil pooped out: Curioso/Shutterstock; P. 155, wolverine:
Stayer/Shutterstock; P. 157, wolverine closeup: Justin Kral/Shutterstock.